D0601717

You Can Write Speeches and Debates

Jennifer Rozines Roy and Johannah Haney

Enslow Publishers, Inc.

40 Industrial Road	PO Box 38
Box 398	Aldershot
Berkeley Heights, NJ 07922	Hants GU12 6BP
USA	UK

http://www.enslow.com

Library of Congress Cataloging-in-Publication Data

Roy, Jennifer Rozines, 1967-
      You can write speeches and debates / Jennifer Rozines Roy and Johannah Haney.
          v. cm. — (You can write)
      Includes bibliographical references and index.
      Contents: You can prepare a speech and debate — All about speeches and debates—
Before you write—You're ready to write—Revising, proofreading, and editing—
Presenting it.
      ISBN 0-7660-2087-8 (hard : alk. paper)
      1. Speechwriting. 2. Debates and debating. [1. Public speaking. 2. Debates and
debating—Juvenile literature.] I. Haney, Johannah. II. Title. III. Series.
      PN4142.R69 2003
      808.5—dc21

                                                                        2003002238

Printed in the United States of America

10 9 8 7 6 5 4 3 2 1

To Our Readers: We have done our best to make sure all Internet Addresses in this book
were active and appropriate when we went to press. However, the author and the
publisher have no control over and assume no liability for the material available on those
Internet sites or on other Web sites they may link to. Any comments or suggestions can
be sent by e-mail to comments@enslow.com or to the address on the back cover.

Illustration Credits: Enslow Publishers, Inc.

Cover Illustration: Enslow Publishers, Inc.

Table of Contents

Chapter One

You Can Prepare a Speech and Debate

Your teacher has just given you an assignment—to give a speech. What is your first response? Do you:

(a) shout "yes!" and pump your fist in the air in excitement, or

(b) feel your heart begin to race, while your hands start to shake and your stomach does flip-flops so violently you are afraid you might throw up?

If you answered (a), that's great! You know that speaking before an audience can be a positive experience. This book will help you learn more about communicating your thoughts and ideas effectively and successfully.

If your answer was (b), you are not alone. Getting up in front of a group of people and speaking can be scary. In fact, public speaking is the number one fear that people have. But almost everyone has to speak in front of an audience at some time. For many, their first public speaking opportunity is at school. Teachers who assign speeches are giving their students the chance to learn valuable skills that will last a lifetime.

Perhaps you have to give a speech. Or you may be participating in a debate, which is a more formal form of public speaking. The first thing you need to know is that public speaking does not have to be difficult. It can even be fun. (Lots of people even choose to do it as a career!) With practice and preparation, even the most nervous person can be a good speaker.

Everybody has something interesting to say. In this book you will learn how to speak about things that are interesting and important to you. You will learn how to say them in a confident, organized way. And when you are finished reading this book, you will hopefully be one of the people who answered (a) to the first question in this chapter.

"Yes!" you'll shout happily. "I get to give a speech!"

Why Give a Speech?

It is important to learn how to communicate a point. Speaking in front of classmates is a great way to practice communication skills. You will use these skills all your life—in school and in your job. Preparing and giving a speech is a great way to voice your opinions or pass on information. In order to present your ideas to people, you need to know how to give an effective speech.

Speech and debate are both great ways to offer your viewpoints to others. But before you do either one, there is a lot of research and writing that must take place. The best public speaker in the world still won't persuade anyone of much without doing some research and writing. In this book, you will learn how to choose a topic and prepare to present that topic either in a speech or a debate before an audience.

Speech

A speech is a prepared talk that aims to either inform (give information) or persuade (convince others of something). Some examples include campaign speeches, acceptance speeches (given by someone who wins an award), and oral reports for school. Speeches can have other goals as well—for example, amusing an audience or moving them emotionally.

Speeches often do more than one thing at a time. For example, when one of your classmates gives a speech to the class about recycling, she is persuading the audience to participate in recycling programs by informing them through the use of facts that support her point. These facts may include the limited availability of landfill space, the possible financial rewards for the school, and the environmental benefits of recycling. All these ideas might help convince the audience to agree with her.

I'd like to thank the Academy for giving me this award.

Best Performance in a Book

As Americans, the right to free speech gives us the chance to express our opinions on any issue in public. Do you think it is important that your classmates and community participate in a recycling program? Are you against school uniforms? Would you make a good class president?

Debate

The issues mentioned above are issues that can also be *debated*. This means that there are two or more different opinions about an issue that can be argued. When people debate an issue, each side gives speeches about its viewpoint. There are very specific rules for a debate that we will talk about later in this book.

Let's look at the issue of school uniforms. One opinion is that all students should be required to wear uniforms to school. Another opinion is that students should be able to wear whatever they want to class. In a debate, each side would take an opposing viewpoint.

In speeches and debates, you have the chance to voice your opinions. But who will listen if you do not prepare an effective speech and debate? That is what we are here to learn—you have the power to make your voice heard.

What Is Persuasive Writing?

We are all exposed to different ideas every day, whether through watching television, reading the newspaper, or talking to friends at school. By observing and experiencing the world around us, we are able to form opinions about everything from what we like on our pizza to who to elect student council treasurer. You will find that many people would like to change your opinion about certain things. To do so, they will need to persuade you to think like they do.

There are many forms of persuasion. You may want to read a new book, for example, but several friends have told you they didn't like it. Would you read it anyway, or would you accept your friends' opinions and choose another? If you decide to read the book, you may form your own idea about whether or not it was worth reading. If not, you'll never know for sure, because you were persuaded to believe it was not a good book.

The editorial section of the newspaper gives people a chance to write and express their opinions on different issues. This is also a form of persuasive writing. You may have had a certain idea about something, and then changed your mind after

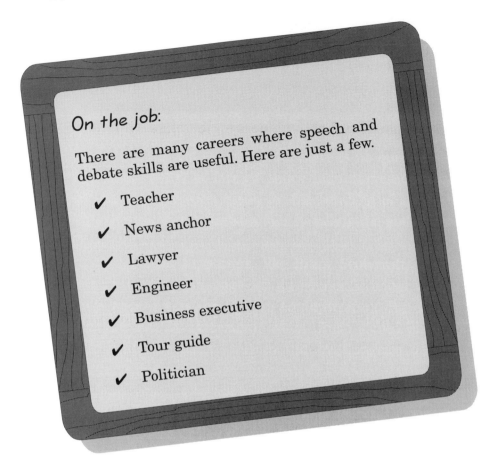

On the job:

There are many careers where speech and debate skills are useful. Here are just a few.

- ✔ Teacher
- ✔ News anchor
- ✔ Lawyer
- ✔ Engineer
- ✔ Business executive
- ✔ Tour guide
- ✔ Politician

reading someone else's opinion on the same topic. In that case, the persuasive writing was successful, because you now think the same thing as the writer. You believe in his or her point of view.

Persuasive writing can take many forms to convince you to think or act in a certain way. The writer uses his opinions to express why he feels his idea is important. He might use information to support his point and encourage you to accept his way of thinking. He can't just tell you to agree with him—he needs to give solid reasons why you should.

A good persuasive writer chooses a topic; takes a position, or side; presents a strong argument for that position; and then provides supporting information to the audience. It takes time to organize and write a persuasive paper. You must be knowledgeable about your topic and research it carefully. The audience must feel your honesty in order to believe your opinions.

The Pros and Cons

Because an opinion is personal, or subjective, another person may not share the same idea. It is important to recognize that there are at least two

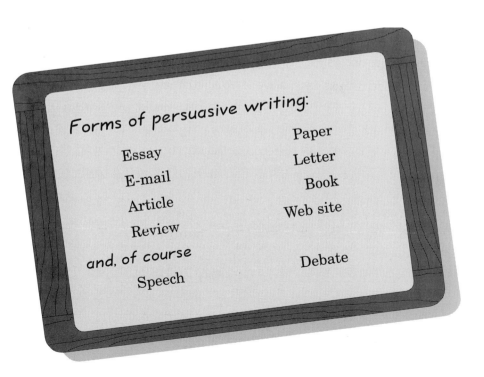

Forms of persuasive writing:

Essay

E-mail

Article

Review

and, of course

Speech

Paper

Letter

Book

Web site

Debate

sides (or pros and cons) to every issue, and it is often impossible to be in total agreement. The *pros* are the points in support of a particular idea; the *cons* are the points against it.

Persuasive writing requires you to provide supporting information when you are presenting your point of view. The person next to you may disagree with you anyway, but he or she can respect your opinion when given the facts. You may not be able to convince someone to change her way of thinking, but she may agree to look at your ideas more closely.

A debate is an excellent example of the idea of pros and cons. In a debate, one side gives the pro side of an argument, and one side gives the con side. Each side provides information to support its position. The winner is the person (or the team) that is able to convince the audience to believe most strongly in his or her ideas. We most often see debates in action during elections, where the candidates spend an evening discussing the issues at hand. You can also join the speech and debate team in high school to practice your persuasion skills.

Fact vs. Opinion

Good persuasive writing requires strong supporting information. It is not enough to just ask the reader or audience to believe what you say— you must give them a reason. You are trying to convince people that your opinion, or idea, is a good one, so you will want to use factual information as well as the opinions of others to prove your point.

How do you tell the difference between fact and opinion? A fact is something that can be or has been proven. We know, for example, that George Washington was the first president of the United States of America. That is a fact. We know our country has fifty states. That is also a fact. A fact is what we know for sure. Your birthday is a fact, and so is your age. You may have brown hair and blue eyes, and that is a fact.

An opinion is what we think about a certain thing. Opinions are our ideas, thoughts, and feelings and cannot be proven. We often start sentences about opinions with "I feel ... I think ... I like." We may be convinced that the soda we like is the best. But that is not a fact, because the person sitting next to us may prefer another brand. You may think baseball is the best sport in America, but your neighbor may prefer football. Those ideas are subject to a person's opinions.

An Outline for Persuasive Writing

The following list will help you create an outline for your persuasive speech or debate.

1. Choose your topic.

2. Take a position, or side—what is the opinion or idea you are trying to get across?

3. Who is your audience?

4. Present a strong argument—how will you persuade your audience?

5. Make a "pros and cons" chart for your argument. How will you respond to the other side?

6. Provide supporting information—research carefully and take notes.

7. Begin writing.

You Can Do It!

Writing a speech can be fun, especially if you choose a topic you like. Start thinking about things that are important to you that others may find interesting. Get together with your classmates to discuss what they think too. This will help you get your audience involved when you give your speech. Take time to prepare and practice your speech carefully. You can be persuasive—just give it a try.

Chapter Two

All About Speeches and Debates

Before we jump into writing our speeches and preparing our debates, let's take a closer look at what exactly makes a speech and a debate.

What Is a Speech?

A speech is a prepared talk given to an audience. We have all heard someone give a speech. Maybe a classmate gave a speech about how he or she will increase class fund-raising efforts during elections for class office. You have probably seen the president give a speech on TV. When someone wins an award, he or she often gives a speech to thank people who helped in the achievement.

Giving a speech during class elections about

how you will benefit the class in a leadership role is aiming to persuade people to vote for you. You are giving your opinion about why you are the best person for the job.

On the other hand, giving a speech about recycling for a class project aims to inform people about the environment. This type of speech would probably include many facts and statistics. We will learn more about statistics later in this chapter.

Many times a speech aims to both inform and persuade. For example, a speech about why students should not do drugs may both inform the audience about the number of drug-related injuries and deaths and then use this information to persuade students to say no to drugs.

What Parts Does a Speech Have?

A speech is organized in much the same way as other forms of writing. It has an introduction, a body, and a conclusion.

The introduction tells your audience what your speech is about. It gets your audience interested in your topic and provides basic background information. You are letting your audience know what you will be talking about in the speech and getting them to want to know more.

The body of a speech discusses your main points, which are the facts and ideas you want your audience to know. Each main point for your topic will have its own section. All of these sections taken together make up the body of your speech. If you are expressing an opinion, it is in the body section that you need to provide support for it. The body is the largest part of your speech.

The conclusion sums up the speech so that the audience remembers the main points. It also reviews why your topic is important.

These elements will be discussed further in Chapter 4.

What Is Included in a Speech?

Speeches include a variety of tools that are designed to communicate information most easily. Because members of the audience cannot re-hear a part of your speech the same way that a reader can re-read a section of an article, speakers use a variety of devices to make the information "stick."

Repetition

Often in a speech, main points are repeated a few times so that the audience has a chance for it to sink in. Of course this doesn't mean that information is repeated over and over again the same way, but when you present the important information in a couple of different ways, the audience has a greater chance of remembering the main points.

Visual Aids

If the format of your speech allows it, visual aids— such as posters, charts, models, and videos—will help your audience remember what you say. They can also add support to a persuasive speech.

Thought-Provoking Questions

Asking your audience questions will get them thinking about areas of your topic they may not have considered. This makes for a more meaningful and memorable speech.

Emotional and Sensory Language

Language that appeals to your audience's emotions will help them become involved in what you are saying. And using colorful words that engage the listeners' senses will make your speech more interesting.

Statistics

A statistic is a number based on a survey, poll, or scientific experiment that gives information about quantity or degree—often in terms of a percentage or proportion. Statistics offer a way to present facts to your audience that hit close to home and make sense.

For instance, it is easy to say that many high school students have tried cigarette smoking. To make this fact more powerful, try using a statistic to illustrate the fact. For example, a statistic that relates to the cigarette smoking fact is, "One out of every three high school students has tried tobacco in the last month." (National Youth Tobacco Survey, 1999)

Sometimes a statistic refers to a general quantity rather than a specific number. An example of this kind of statistic is, "Each year, smoking kills more people than AIDS, alcohol, drug abuse, car crashes, murders, suicides, and fires—combined!" (Centers for Disease Control, 2001)

When you use a statistic in a speech, it is important to say where you found the statistic so that your speech is credible. (Credible means believable or trustworthy.) If you got a statistic about smoking from a tobacco company, it would be less reliable, because tobacco companies have reasons to downplay the number of teen smokers. On the other hand, if your statistic came from the U.S. Centers for Disease Control or another government or medical source, your audience will trust the statistic more. By using reliable sources for facts and statistics, your speech gains strength. We will talk more about reliable sources in Chapter 3.

What Is a Debate?

One of the most structured types of speech communication is the debate. A debate is a formal discussion in which each side presents opposing answers to a question. Used by Congress, state and local government, and even our presidential candidates, debates are a way to resolve issues and solve problems.

You have probably been involved in an informal debate yourself without realizing it. For example, if you argue for or against a new dress code at school, discuss your opinions on environmental issues, or tell why you nominated your favorite teacher for an award, you are engaged in an informal debate.

Lawyers engage in a type of debate every time

they enter the courtroom. Although the outcome may differ from a formal debate because the guilt or innocence of the defendant is at stake, lawyers follow many of the rules of debate and present their case to a judge or jury, who then considers the case as presented by both sides. If you have ever thought about a career in law, developing strong debate skills is very important.

Participating in a debate helps sharpen your organizational, writing, and public speaking skills. Preparing a speech for debate requires careful research and thinking. You will learn how to express your opinions in a way that may successfully influence others to see your side of the story. You will also become more aware of the issues in the world around you and learn how to respond to them. As you become more confident as a public speaker, you may choose to join a club devoted to debate.

Many employers and colleges are looking for students with strong oral presentation skills. Those skills are what you use in debate. People with strong oral presentation skills are thought of as natural leaders by many employers and are often promoted faster in their jobs.

Many high schools and colleges have debate teams that compete in tournaments on the local, state, and national levels. The art of competitive speech and debate is called *forensics*. It is different from the type of forensics used in courts of law, though both words have their root in the term "forum," as in a place for public discussion.

What Is Included in a Debate?

A formal debate, such as one that a high school debate team might participate in, has precise rules and formats to follow.

Every debate begins with a *proposition*: a statement, usually calling for change on an issue. The proposition must be such that each side can take a stand on whether to agree or disagree. The proposition always starts with the word "Resolved."

For example, the proposition may read as follows, "Resolved: That schools should require students to perform community service." The two competing teams are assigned either the *affirmative* or the *negative* view. The affirmative view is *for* the proposition; the negative view is *against* it.

In competitive debating, each debater is assigned either the affirmative or negative position for each competition. For different competitions, however, a debater might be assigned a different position to debate.

The team members in a debate must first research and explore the subject before writing their speeches for debate. They gather facts and evidence to support their side and carefully construct responses to arguments they think the other side may make. Depending on the debate format, the team prepares a series of speeches to be given in a certain amount of time. The members of the team rehearse their speeches several times in preparation for the formal debate.

Resolved: That "salmon loaf surprise" should be removed from the cafeteria menu!

How Does a Debate Take Place?

There are three different formats for a formal debate. Regardless of which format is used, there are enforced time limits. The speaker is not permitted to continue after his or her time runs out for that segment. The selected format is strictly followed so as not to give one team an advantage over the other. There must be an equal number of debaters on each team, and each team receives an equal amount of time to debate the issue during the competition.

Each speaking team member gives a speech with supporting facts and evidence in the first half of the debate. These are called *constructive speeches*. This is the best chance to prove the point before the judge. The *rebuttal* takes place in the second half of the debate, and provides each team with a chance to ask questions and give the other team a chance to reply in the next segment. There is no speaking out of turn by either team.

Affirmative or negative?

Think about the affirmative and the negative positions on the propositions below. Discuss with your classmates how you would argue for or against them.

1. Money for art education should be cut to free more money for subjects like math, science, and reading.

2. Schools should charge a fine when students break major rules, such as the rule against smoking cigarettes.

3. Students should be required to attend school until age 18.

4. The local government should require citizens to recycle common materials, like aluminum cans and newspapers.

5. Every citizen over the age of 18 should be legally required to vote in all elections.

Let's learn more about each of the three types of debate format.

Lincoln-Douglas Debate Format

The first type of debate is called the Lincoln-Douglas debate. This is one of the most common types of debate. It is named for Abraham Lincoln and Stephen Douglas, who used this format to debate the issue of slavery in the United States in

Terms in a debate:

1. **Proposition:** the issue being debated.

2. **Constructive speech:** the speech in which both sides present their initial arguments.

3. **Rebuttal:** the act of disagreeing by offering an argument against each point of the opponent's argument.

4. **Cross-examination:** to question a person closely about information that person has provided.

5. **Affirmative:** the side that argues *for* the proposition.

6. **Negative:** the side that argues *against* the proposition.

1858. In a Lincoln-Douglas debate, there is one debater for the affirmative side and one debater for the negative side. The following chart shows how the Lincoln-Douglas debate is done.

Part of debate	Time
Affirmative constructive speech	6 minutes
Negative cross-examination	3 minutes
Negative constructive speech	7 minutes
Affirmative cross-examination	3 minutes
First affirmative rebuttal	4 minutes
Negative rebuttal	6 minutes
Second affirmative rebuttal	3 minutes

Policy Debate Format

In a policy debate, each side has two debaters. The affirmative side must prove four things:

- significance: the assigned issue is a problem

- inherency: the problem needs a solution

- solvency: your solution will solve that problem

- advantages: the solution has clear advantages over the present state of the problem

The negative side must try to show that the affirmative side is wrong about one of the four requirements above. If the negative side can prove just one of these wrong, they win the debate. The following chart shows the format of the policy debate.

Part of debate	Time
First affirmative constructive speech	8 minutes
Cross-examination by second negative speaker	3 minutes
First negative constructive speech	8 minutes
Cross-examination by first affirmative speaker	3 minutes
Second affirmative construction speech	8 minutes
Cross-examination by first negative speaker	3 minutes
Second negative constructive speech	8 minutes
Cross-examination by second affirmative speaker	3 minutes
Rebuttal by first negative speaker	4 minutes
Rebuttal by first affirmative speaker	4 minutes
Rebuttal by second negative speaker	4 minutes
Rebuttal by second affirmative speaker	4 minutes

Parliamentary Debate Format

There are two debaters in both the affirmative and negative positions in a parliamentary debate, and each team member gives one constructive speech. After the constructive speeches are made, members of the audience are chosen randomly to make a one-minute speech in support of either side, called a *floor speech*. The debaters then present their rebuttals based on the floor speeches. After the debate, the audience members vote to decide the winner. Here is how a parliamentary debate is done:

Part of debate	Time
First affirmative constructive speech	8 minutes
First negative constructive speech	8 minutes
Second affirmative construction speech	8 minutes
Second negative constructive speech	8 minutes
Six one-minute floor speeches	6 minutes
Negative rebuttal	4 minutes
Affirmative rebuttal	4 minutes

Judging Debates

When the debaters are done speaking, it is time for the judges to make their decision. Judges are the people who decide the outcome of the debate. They consider who has taken the strongest position with the best supporting facts, and whether the other team's questions were answered. There are no tie situations—a winner is always chosen.

Every debater knows that you win some and you lose some. Even when you don't win, you learn valuable speaking, research, and thinking skills. The more you debate, the more confident you will get. In the meantime, enjoy yourself! Debating can be challenging and fun.

Preparing for a Debate

There are some questions you must ask yourself before beginning a debate. First, what is the issue that you will be debating? Next, list three or four points for the proposition and then another three or four points against it. It is important to consider both sides of the issue, no matter which one you agree with. After all, you may not be assigned to the side of the debate that reflects your opinion. Think of the strongest arguments that you might expect from the opposing side. How will you defend yourself against these arguments?

Once you've considered these points, you are well on your way to a convincing debate.

Other Types of Competitive Speaking

There are three main types of competitive forensics events in addition to debate: spontaneous, original, and interpretive.

Spontaneous means "unplanned." There are two types of spontaneous speaking. In *extemporaneous* speaking, contestants choose from three topics, do half an hour of timed research, then deliver a 5–7 minute speech on the topic. In *impromptu* speaking, contestants have two minutes to prepare a five-minute speech on a thought-provoking quotation or question.

Original speeches include *oratory*, *advocacy*, *prose-poetry*, and *expository*, all written, memorized, and performed by the contestant.

Interpretive speaking, in which the contestant presents the work of others, includes *dramatic interpretation*, *humorous interpretation*, *thematic interpretation*, and *oratorical interpretation*.

Ask your teacher for more information on these types of forensics events. If you were going to compete in one of these events, which would you choose? Why?

Chapter Three

Before You Write a Speech

Now that you are familiar with speeches and debates, it is time to begin writing. This chapter discusses how to prepare and write a speech. But this information can be useful for those who are preparing a debate too. Every debate begins with an opening statement called a constructive speech that, like other speeches, must be researched and written before you go before your audience.

You might have an assignment to write a speech for school, or maybe you are running for student council and want to make a big splash with your candidate speech.

Whatever your speech or debate is for, you *can* write and prepare an extraordinary one.

Choosing Your Topic

How do you decide on a topic for your speech? Sometimes figuring this out is easy. For example, if you are preparing a speech to give classmates when you are running for class president, you will have a pretty good idea of what the topic of your speech will be. Other times, your teacher might assign the topic.

But even when choosing the topic seems simple, it is important to make sure that the scope of your topic is manageable. The *scope* of a topic is how broad or narrow the topic is.

For example, if you are assigned to give a speech on school uniforms, the basic topic is determined for you. However, the scope of this topic is far too broad for a speech. There is no way you could talk about all the important aspects of this topic in one speech.

Hmmm ... I think my topic is too narrow.

Does this mean your teacher gave you a bad topic? Not at all! In fact, this gives you a lot of freedom in determining the scope of your topic. In this case, you will have to narrow your topic.

You should start by asking yourself a few questions: What about school uniforms is most interesting to you? What are some different opinions people have about school uniforms? Do you know anyone who has to wear a uniform to school? What does he or she think about it?

What is your opinion about requiring students to wear school uniforms? This should give you a good start on narrowing your topic.

But what if there is no topic assigned for your speech? Then you have even more freedom in determining your topic. Again, ask yourself some questions to get started.

When you feel you have a good topic, talk to your classmates, friends, parents, and teachers about the different ideas you have about narrowing your topic. Many times this will help you fine-tune your topic.

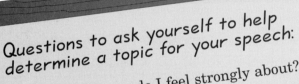

Questions to ask yourself to help determine a topic for your speech:

✔ What issues do I feel strongly about?

✔ What subjects in the news are interesting to me?

✔ What are some topics that are popular for students to talk about during free time?

✔ What topics has my favorite magazine been talking about?

Audience and Style

It is important to know who will be in your audience when you are giving a speech. Why, you ask? Think of it this way: When you talk in normal conversation to your friends, you probably use different language (slang, for example), tone of voice, and body language than when you talk to your teacher or principal. These differences cross over into giving a speech too.

If you are giving a speech as a candidate for class office, your topic, research, style, and delivery will be geared toward your classmates. But if you are giving a speech to the parent-teacher organization about how students can help with fund-raising activities, your research and style will need to be appropriate for adults.

Once you have figured out who your audience is, you can determine what style you will use in writing your speech. If your audience is your peers, you are probably familiar with what kinds of examples and words they will understand and relate to best.

But if your audience is not your peers, make sure to think carefully about what writing and speaking style will be most successful with that audience. You will also have to consider the content of the speech. What might matter about recycling for your peers may be very different from what matters for teachers or parents. Consider how the content might differ depending on the audience. (See the example on the next page.)

Another thing to consider is how much background information your audience has about

Audience		
	Teachers	**Classmates**	**Kindergartners**
Examples of ways to recycle:	Teachers can recycle by taking turns bringing in the newspaper to the teachers' lounge.	We can recycle by having an aluminum can drive to raise money for our class field trip.	Kindergartners can recycle by using both sides of the paper for drawing and writing.

your topic. If you are giving a speech about the environment, it is usually safe to assume that your audience will realize why preserving the environment is important. Even if you think your audience will have some knowledge about the topic, be sure not to assume that they will know as much as you. If your speech is about something less well known, you will need to give more background detail.

Main Points

Before you begin your research and writing, you need to identify what the main points of the speech will be. This means deciding what you want to inform or persuade your audience about. Your speech will focus on these points.

For example, if you are giving a speech about the benefit of requiring school uniforms, your main points might be:

1. Requiring school uniforms cuts down on misbehavior among students.

2. School uniforms help parents save money.

3. School uniforms help break down status differences among students, since everyone wears the same thing.

Most speeches will have about two or three main points plus supporting details. This keeps the scope of your topic under control. If you have too many key points, you might consider whether you need to narrow the scope of your topic.

So, how do you decide what your main points are? Think about what issues made you decide to select your topic. Brainstorm a list of the different elements of your topic.

Do Your Research and Take Good Notes

Now that you have a topic and key points, it's time to hit the library and do some research. It is important to use good, reliable resources to do your research so that you build credibility with your audience.

The key to your speech is choosing good points.

Encyclopedias are a good place to start to get the most basic information about your topic, but you will need to get more in-depth sources as well. Newspapers and magazines offer interesting and helpful statistics about many topics that deal with current events such as the environment, politics, and

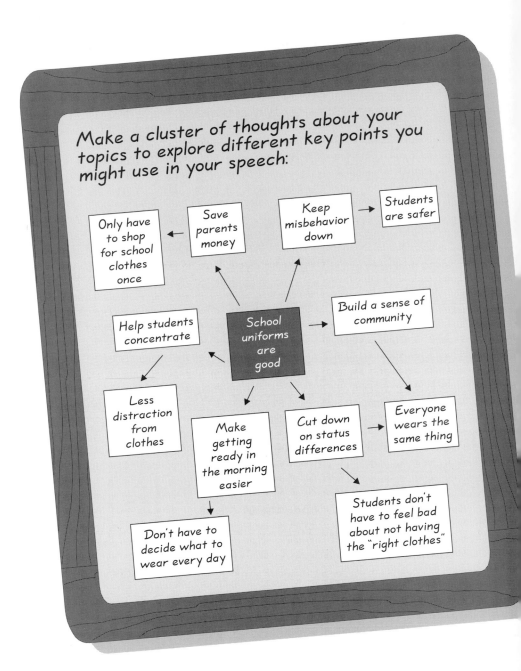

Make a cluster of thoughts about your topics to explore different key points you might use in your speech:

schools. Ask your librarian for help finding articles in newspapers and magazines.

Many students also use the Internet to do research. The Internet can be a great resource; however, you have to be careful to make sure the Internet source is reliable. Because anyone can put information on the Internet, a lot of the information there is simply wrong.

You can tell who is behind a Web site by looking at the suffix in the site's name. A commercial site has **.com** in its name. Be very careful about information from .com sites. Sites with **.org** usually offer good information, but they also present an organization's point of view. Sites with **.gov** (government sites) and **.edu** (college and university sites) provide reliable information.

If you are not sure whether a Web site is offering credible information, see if you can find similar information elsewhere. Ask a teacher, a parent, or your librarian for help.

As you do your research, take notes when you come across information that will be valuable in writing your speech. The more detailed and organized your notes are, the easier it will be to write your speech. Here are a few hints when you are taking notes:

- Keep separate pages, or even separate notebooks, for information you find about your different main points. Using note cards to make your notes can help you organize your research when you begin to write.

- Use a highlighter or different colored pens to organize your thoughts within your notes.

- Be sure to make a note saying where you find each piece of information. Chances are you will need to refer to the same source later, and you will be able to find it easily. And even though you will not be citing sources the same way you would for a research paper, you need to be able to show you have not plagiarized any of your material (copied it from someone else).

Make an Outline

Organizing your notes into an outline will make the process of writing your speech even easier. If you used separate notebooks or different colored pens for your different key points, use that as your starting point. If you have not separated your notes yet, try it now.

Think about what sequence will make the most sense for your key points. If you are having trouble deciding what order to put your key points in, try different visualization techniques. Write out each key point on a note card and pin them on a bulletin board in different sequences. See what makes the most sense to you. Get an opinion from a teacher, a parent, or a friend. Many good speechwriters choose to put the most important or persuasive point last in the speech. Your audience is likely to remember the last part of your speech the most.

Your outline might look something like this:

   I. Introduction

  II. Main Point 1. *School uniforms help parents save money.*

      A. Talk a little about the background of this key point

      B. Research fact #1

         1. The importance of this fact

      C. Research fact #2

         1. The importance of this fact

 III. Main point 2. *Requiring school uniforms cuts down on misbehavior among students.*

      A. Talk a little about the background of this key point

      B. Research fact #1

         1. The importance of this fact

      C. Research fact #2

         1. The importance of this fact

      D. Research Fact #3

         1. The importance of this fact

  IV. Main Point 3. *School uniforms help break down status differences among students, since everyone wears the same thing.*

      A. Talk a little about the background of this key point

      B. Research fact #1

         1. The importance of this fact

      C. Research fact #2

         1. The importance of this fact

      D. Research Fact #3

         1. The importance of this fact

  V. Conclusion

Visual Aids

Visual aids are things for the audience to look at. They help explain or show information. Examples of visual aids include charts, tables, figures, pictures, three-dimensional models, and videos. If you are giving a speech about the history of hats in America, for example, you could bring in pictures from magazines of hats throughout history as well as charts that show the rising popularity of wearing hats. In fact, you could even bring in some actual hats to show the audience.

Many people learn by seeing facts as well as hearing them. While it is interesting to hear that seventy-four out of one hundred people agree with your key point, it is even more impressive to see a chart showing this fact.

If you use visual aids, make sure they are easy to read and big enough for everyone in the room to see. Remember not to stand in front of your visual aids or no one will see them. Keep your visual aids simple, with large type and clear illustrations. Remember, the idea is to make the information easier to understand, not more difficult.

You should also keep in mind that visual aids are an option, not a necessity. In

Why use visual aids during a speech?

✔ To get your message across to your audience more clearly

✔ To save time explaining statistics

✔ To encourage your audience to pay attention

✔ To help you stay calm

✔ To keep your speech on target

fact, you might not be permitted to use visual aids in a speech assigned by your teacher. Other times you will be required to use visual aids. Visual aids are not allowed in formal debates, and they are only permitted in the expository speaking section of forensics competitions.

Chapter Four

You're Ready to Write

Your topic is chosen, your research done, and now you even have an outline and sequence for your main points. Time to start writing. You'll start by writing a rough draft, which you can then revise until it is in its final form.

Writing a Rough Draft

Drafting is the process of putting words down on paper (or in a computer). A rough draft is a first attempt at writing your speech. Writing a rough draft is an important part of the process of preparing your speech. Don't worry about making mistakes while writing a rough draft. Just try to get your facts and ideas written down so that they make sense. Not even the most talented writers can get everything perfect on the first try. You will have a chance to fine-tune and perfect your rough draft later.

When you are writing a rough draft, try to get your main points down in the order that they will be in for your final draft. Once your research is in the format of a written speech, you can polish the details to make the best speech possible.

So what is the format of a speech? Like many other kinds of writing, a speech starts with an introduction, moves to the body sections, where your key points are discussed, and ends with a conclusion that ties everything together. Let's take a closer look at each of these parts of a speech.

The Introduction

The opening of your speech should capture your audience's attention and get them interested in your topic. The opening is called the *lead*. Consider the following two leads:

1. "Our society uses too much paper. That is why recycling paper is important."

2. "Every week, more than half a million trees are cut down to make newspapers . . . and two-thirds of those papers are never recycled." (Environmental Defense)

Which lead is better? The first lead is general and dull. The second one opens with a surprising statistic that makes you want to learn more, so that makes it the better lead. Beginning with a

Make your opening POWERFUL!

powerful statement will engage your audience's interest and make them eager to hear more from you.

Next, give some background information about your topic. The background information you provide should explain your main points. If the main point of your speech is to inform about recycling and persuade your audience to participate in recycling, you might give brief background information about the many programs designed to help people recycle in their everyday lives.

The last part of your opening should list the main points of your speech. Obviously you do not need to go into any detail about your main points in the introduction, but stating them in the introduction will help your audience listen for them during your speech and remember them afterward.

The Body

The body of your speech is the largest part. Each section of the body discusses the main points and gives supportive details. Each section should be about just one point.

Let's say your topic is the need for music programs in schools. Your first body section could tell about the studies that show that students who take musical instrument lessons get higher scores on reading and math tests. Your second body section could discuss the importance of music to different cultures. A third body section might focus on how giving young people the opportunity to perform and express themselves musically increases their self-confidence and self-esteem.

Each section should give research, details, and possibly opinions about each of these main points. You would then continue to write until you have no more key points to tell. Remember to include in the body where you got information and what it is based on. In giving proper credit, you gain credibility.

The Closing

After you have discussed every main point, it is time to give the closing. The closing of your speech brings the audience back to each point briefly and ties them all together. You should not introduce any new information or points in your conclusion. Just remind the audience of all the main ideas you want them to know and remember.

The closing ties it all up.

For example, a speech whose aim is to persuade the audience that music lessons in schools are worth the money spent on the programs might conclude like this:

> *Music lessons are important in schools because they help students score better on standardized tests, help students learn culture through music, and give students a chance to perform and gain self-esteem. Even though a lot of schools get rid of music programs because of money problems, the benefits of music education make up for the cost. If we can keep our music programs, we might have even more great musicians in the next generation.*

You're Almost There!

Now your rough draft should look something like this:

  I. Opening
  II. Body
      A. Key Point #1
          1. Research supporting key point #1
      B. Key Point #2
          1. Research supporting key point #2
      C. Key Point #3
          1. Research supporting key point #3
  III. Closing

There are just a few more steps until your speech is ready: revising, editing, and proofreading your speech and preparing your presentation.

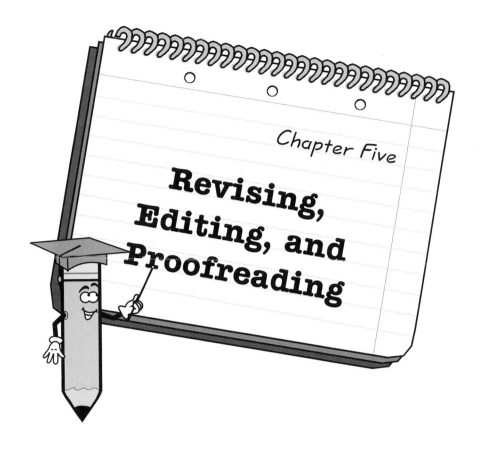

Chapter Five

Revising, Editing, and Proofreading

With your rough draft complete, it is time to revise, edit, and proofread. Once you have done these three things, you will have a second draft. You might even do more and have a third draft. When you feel you have made every correction necessary to make a great speech, you have reached your final draft.

It is important to note the difference between revising, editing, and proofreading. *Revising* is making changes to the information in your writing—for example, taking out a main point or adding a research source. *Editing* is making sure that each sentence, paragraph, and section is clear, makes sense, and is appropriate to your audience. *Proofreading* means correcting spelling, grammar, and punctuation.

All of these are important to making your speech magnificent. However, you will work most efficiently if you start with revising, and then move to editing, and finally proofreading. After all, if you proofread everything, then later decide to replace a whole section with different information, you will have spent time proofreading material that is not in your final speech.

Revising

The first step toward a final draft is revising your rough draft. Now is the time to read the words you have written and to ask yourself a few questions to see what kinds of revisions you will need.

Revise! Edit! Proof!
Revise! Edit! Proof!

1. Does my opening paragraph introduce my topic?

2. Do the main points in the body support my topic?

3. Would adding or taking out information help make my speech better?

4. Does the order of my paragraphs make sense?

If you know you need revisions but are having a hard time seeing how to revise, make an outline of your rough draft. Compare it to the outline you made from your notes before you started writing. How are they the same/different? Can you identify where you got off track? Sometimes revising your outline first will help your rough draft make more sense.

Editing

Once your revisions are complete, it is time to start editing. Editing is making sure that each sentence, paragraph, and section is clear, makes sense, and is appropriate to your audience. In any kind of writing, each sentence, paragraph, and section has a purpose, or goal. For example, the goal of the following sentence is to inform about the current state of student life:

> *Today's student is facing a variety of pressures from peers, family, and extracurricular obligations.*

When you edit your rough draft, you are making sure that each sentence, paragraph, and section is successful in fulfilling its goal. Look at each individual sentence: Will your audience understand the goal of the sentence? Is there a better way that you can phrase the sentence? Do the same with each paragraph and each section.

Proofreading

Proofreading is reading the text to make sure that the spelling, grammar, and punctuation are all correct. It may not seem important to have correct spelling and punctuation in a speech. But written errors may turn into errors in pronunciation and delivery—and you don't want those! Sometimes it is hard to focus on these issues when you are reading your speech because you are focusing on the information alone. You

Careful editing will help you reach your goal.

may want to ask another person with good proofreading skills to check for mistakes.

The Final Draft

Now that your revising, editing, and proofreading work is complete, you are one step away from having a completed final draft. Before you declare it complete, read your speech aloud a few times. Listen for awkward-sounding words or sentences and places where your audience might get confused. Time yourself so you know if your speech meets requirements set by your teacher or the debate format you are using. Make sure you are speaking in a slow and understandable voice. If your speech is running long or short, go back and revise it to make it the appropriate length.

Once you have read your speech aloud to yourself, assemble a small audience of your classmates, family members, or friends and read your speech to them. Ask your practice audience to make notes about places in your speech where more information is needed, where information is unclear, or where things get a little confusing. After your speech, have a group discussion about these notes. You will get a better sense of how your speech is working with an audience, and you will identify the places where you can make your speech better.

Has your speech passed the practice audience test? You now officially have a final draft of your speech. Congratulations! Now it's time to practice and prepare for the actual presentation of the speech.

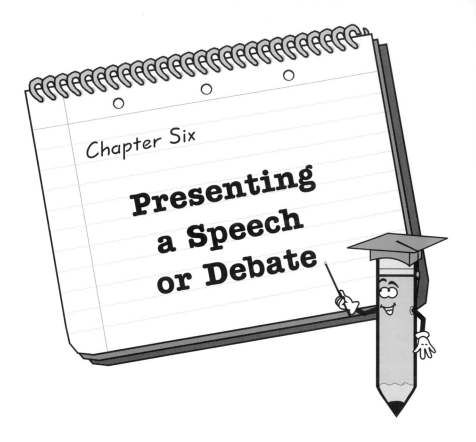

Chapter Six

Presenting a Speech or Debate

Now that your research is done and your speech is written and ready to go, it is time to prepare for your audience. Whether you are giving your speech to a class or in a debate format, you will want to practice the presentation and prepare ways to make it clear and persuasive.

If you have written your speech well, it will be persuasive all on its own. However, a persuasive presentation will drive your main points home and convince your audience even more of your viewpoint. Achieving a persuasive presentation involves being calm, confident, and mindful of presentation skills.

How to Speak for an Audience

How exactly do you go about giving a speech? One of the first issues is deciding what to bring with you in front of your audience. You will want to have all your visual aids ready, of course. But what about the speech you have written?

Sometimes you will need to bring the whole speech with you and read directly from it, but it is usually more effective to just bring notes of your written speech so that you can make eye contact with your audience. You might feel safer bringing the entire written speech in case you lose your train of thought. But if you do this, it is tempting to simply read your speech—and that can be boring for your audience. By just bringing notes, you can connect with your audience better and still have your information available.

There are a few ways to make good notes for your presentation, but one of the best ways is to make an outline of your final draft. This way, all of your key points are laid out in the right order. You can give your speech from the outline or use note cards containing your notes.

You might want to also bring a sheet of your references with you. If an audience member wants to know your source on a specific fact, you will have it readily available.

Beating the Nerves

Many people feel butterflies in their stomach at the mere thought of getting up in front of people. You may fear making a mistake, freezing up, or embarrassing yourself.

You are not alone. Almost everyone has felt this way at some time. The key is to find techniques that work to calm you down so that you can focus on being persuasive to your audience.

First of all, take time the night before your speech or debate to organize your notes, visual aids, and anything else you will need for your presentation. Knowing everything is ready will go a long way in making you feel confident.

One thing you may find helpful is to think back to other speakers you have listened to. You probably wanted them to do well and thought of their efforts positively, even if they were not perfect speakers. Remember that your audience wants you to succeed. Try thinking of them as being on your side—it can help you feel calmer.

Bye-bye, butterflies!

There are some simple things you can do to settle your nerves just before you give a presentation. About ten minutes before your speech or debate, start taking deep, calming breaths. Imagine yourself in front of your audience giving a fabulous presentation. Relax your muscles by flexing and then relaxing them. Slowly count back from one hundred to keep your mind off being nervous.

When it is time for your speech, approach the front of the room calmly and slowly. Take a moment or two to gather your thoughts and take a couple of deep breaths when you reach the front. The most important thing to remember is to take your time. Chances are, time seems to be moving a lot more slowly in your mind, and what feels like an eternity to you is actually just a few moments. But those few moments will mean the difference between appearing calm and collected and looking frazzled.

Speaking Skills

Good speaking skills are a vital part of a winning debate or successful speech. The ability to connect with your audience will help you persuade your audience to believe in your key points.

So, how can you connect with your audience? There are a few surefire ways to do this. One is to make eye contact with members of your audience regularly. It might feel less scary to always be looking down at your notes; however, you will have a much more successful speech if you look at your audience. You will be surprised at how

Tips to beat the jitters:

✔ Take deep, slow breaths.

✔ Imagine yourself giving a magnificent presentation.

✔ Organize your materials well beforehand.

✔ Don't be frightened by your audience.

✔ Take your time.

✔ Have fun.

calming it is to see that your audience is interested in what you are saying.

Use body language to engage your audience. Try not to stand stiffly behind a podium, playing with your hair or nervously adjusting your clothes or eyeglasses. Instead, use the same hand gestures and facial expressions that you would in natural conversation. This will put your audience at ease and allow them to focus on what you are saying. Remember: Your audience *wants* you to do a good job.

Another way to connect with your audience is to show enthusiasm. Let them know that you are excited about your topic and they will be, too. Enthusiasm is catching!

Using your voice well will also help to put your audience at ease. One major fear people have when speaking in front of an audience is that their voice will be shaky or even crack. If you think that your voice sounds shaky, take a deep breath and talk a little louder (just make sure not to shout). Many times, a shaky voice is a timid voice, and turning up the volume a notch can help you sound stronger. If your voice cracks, just ignore it and move on. Chances are that no one else noticed.

One of the most important aspects of good speaking skills is the volume of your voice. After all, how can you give a good speech if your audience cannot hear you? If you know you have a quiet voice, practice speaking more loudly before you give your speech. Sometimes using a microphone is a good solution. If the microphone is

Make sure your audience hears every word!

in its stand, make sure it is at a comfortable height so you do not need to stoop down or stand on your tiptoes to reach it. Ask for help if you need a hand adjusting the height. Make sure it is turned on, and speak several inches from the microphone. Whether you are using a microphone or not, feel free to ask the audience whether they can hear you before you give your speech. Just say, "Can everyone hear me well?" If they cannot, you will know to speak up or adjust the microphone.

Use your voice to keep your audience interested. If you are speaking in a monotone (a single tone of voice), your audience will likely grow bored. Make sure to vary the tone of your voice. Imagine that you are speaking in a conversation with somebody, rather than in front of a group of people.

One mistake made by many novice speakers is speaking too fast. *Slow down!* Even if it seems as slow as molasses to you, it won't sound that way to your audience—it will enable them to follow what you are saying and remember it more easily. Use pauses to emphasize an important word or to set off an important sentence from the rest of your speech. Vary the pace of your speech too—this will help keep your audience interested.

Two other methods can help you improve your speaking style: listening and doing! Listening to recorded speeches of great orators—such as Dr. Martin Luther King, Jr., or John F. Kennedy—can show you what great speaking style is like. And practice on your own is very important. Try videotaping (or audiotaping) yourself, and then

Tips to keep your audience interested:

✔ Make eye contact regularly.

✔ Use confident body language.

✔ Show enthusiasm.

✔ Vary your tone of voice.

✔ Stand with good posture.

✔ Speak loudly and clearly.

watch and listen to the result. This will show you how you can improve and give you extra practice in making your speech.

Questions and Cross-examination

Often, after you have finished a speech, the audience will have an opportunity to ask questions about your speech and key points. In a debate, this comes in the form of a cross-examination. This is a good chance for you to make sure that the audience has absorbed the key points of your speech.

Because you have no way of knowing what questions people will ask, you must improvise during this time. *Improvising* is thinking of an answer as you go along, with no preparation.

Sound scary? It doesn't have to be. Improvising is an exciting activity that will help sharpen your communication skills greatly. When you are improvising, make sure to answer in words that your audience will understand. For example, if your audience is your classmates, you do not want to use fancy or difficult words during the question/answer period. On the other hand, if your audience is a group of adults, you don't want to speak the same way you would while hanging out with your buddies.

During the question/answer period, you will draw on all of your research to form responses, not just the information included in your speech. For example, if your speech is about local recycling, an audience member might ask if the same statistics are true nationwide. Chances are, this information was not in your speech, since it focused on local statistics. But you might remember from your research that national trends were very similar to the local trends.

Improvising? Nothing to it!

Often it is possible to prepare for the question period beforehand. Think about questions that might arise and what your answers might be. After you practice your speech in front of others, find out what questions they have. The questions might not be the same ones that you are asked at your presentation, but they will help you feel more ready for whatever comes your way.

What do you do if you do not know the answer to the question that is asked? Never fear, just about everyone who has ever given a speech or debated has been faced with this. It is okay if you don't know the answer to a question asked. You might say, "I don't know the exact answer to that question, but perhaps later you or I could find it out." After your speech is over, lead that audience member to some of your research sources that might help.

After Your Presentation Is Over

It's done. Congratulations! You have completed your speech! What comes next?

Chances are you will have another speech to prepare at some point. Ask your teacher or a trusted friend who was in the audience to provide some feedback on your speech. Were your main points presented clearly? Did the information flow in a good order? How was the presentation? Where do you have room for improvement? This will help you focus on areas where you can grow stronger for your next speech.

Make sure you congratulate yourself. You did a very brave thing by getting up in front of an audience to share your ideas and opinions. This will become a very important skill in your life. Taking the time to prepare well and make your speech the best it can be will pay off when it comes time to give another speech; you will know just how to approach it.

Giving a speech is one of the most effective ways to voice your opinions about the issues that matter to you. Remember: You *can* make your voice heard.

Glossary

cons—Arguments against a particular position.

cross-examine—To question a person closely about information that person has provided.

debate—A formal discussion in which each side presents opposing answers to a question.

forensics—The science of persuasive speaking; often refers to competitive speech and debate.

persuasive writing—A type of writing that uses opinions to express key points.

plagiarize—To use someone else's words or ideas without giving them credit.

proposition—The issue being debated.

pros—Arguments supporting a particular position.

rebuttal—The act of disagreeing by offering an opposing viewpoint on an issue.

scope—How broad or narrow a topic is.

statistic—A number based on a survey, poll, or scientific experiment that gives information about quantity or degree.

visual aids—Instructional tools such as charts, graphs, or posters that help illustrate information in your speech.

Further Reading

Books

Bennett, William H. *Beginning Debate*. Taos, N.M.: Championship Debate Enterprises, 1995.

Daley, Patrick, and Michael S. Dahlie. *50 Debate Prompts for Kids*. New York: Scholastic, 2001.

Kushner, Malcolm. *Public Speaking For Dummies*®. Indianapolis: Hungry Minds, Inc., 1999.

McManus, Judith A. *How to Write and Deliver an Effective Speech*. Indianapolis: Arco Publishing, 1998.

Sprague, Jo, and Douglas Stuart. *The Speaker's Handbook*. Stamford, Conn.: International Thomson Publishing, 2000.

Internet Addresses

Effective Speech Writing
<http://7-12educators.about.com/library/weekly/aa050900a.htm?oncc=true&>

National Junior Forensics League
<http://debate.uvm.edu/NFL/njfl.html>

Toastmasters International
<http://www.toastmasters.org>

Index